How Product Managers Can Use Better Communication To Boost Sales

How Product Managers Can Use Communication Skills To Make Their Product A Success

"Practical, proven examples of how to use your marketing skills to make your product a success!"

Dr. Jim Anderson

Published by:
Blue Elephant Consulting
Tampa, Florida

Copyright © 2017 by Dr. Jim Anderson

All rights reserved. No part of this book may be reproduced of transmitted in any form or by any means, electronic or mechanical, including photocopying, recording or by any information storage and retrieval system without written permission of the publisher, except for inclusion of brief quotations in a review.

Printed in the United States of America

Library of Congress Control Number: 2017900348

ISBN-13: 978-1542465472

ISBN-10: 1542465478

Warning – Disclaimer

The purpose of this book is to educate and entertain. This book does not promise or guarantee that anyone following the ideas, tips, suggestions, techniques or strategies will be successful. The author, publisher and distributor(s) shall have neither liability nor responsibility to anyone with respect to any loss or damage caused, or alleged to be caused, directly or indirectly by the information contained in this book.

Recent Books By The Author

Product Management

- Managing Your Product Manager Career: How Product Managers Can Find And Succeed In The Right Job

- How Product Managers Can Sell More Of Their Product: Tips & Techniques For Product Managers To Better Understand How To Sell Their Product

Public Speaking

- How To Organize A Speech In Order To Make Your Point: How to put together a speech that will capture and hold your audience's attention

- Changing How You Speak To Overcome Your Fear Of Speaking: Change techniques that will transform a speech into a memorable event

CIO Skills

- New IT Technology Issues Facing CIOs: How CIOs Can Stay On Top Of The Changes In The Technology That Powers The Company

- Keeping The Barbarians Out: How CIOs Can Secure Their Department and Company: Tips And Techniques For CIOs To Use In Order To Secure Both Their IT

Department And Their Company

IT Manager Skills

- How IT Managers Can Use New Technology To Meet Today's IT Challenges: Technologies That IT Managers Can Use In Order to Make Their Teams More Productive

- How To Build High Performance IT Teams: Tips And Techniques That IT Managers Can Use In Order To Develop Productive Teams

Negotiating

- Getting What You Want In A Negotiation By Learning How To Signal: How To Develop The Skill Of Effective Signaling In A Negotiation In Order To Get The Best Possible Outcome

- Exploring How To Get The Deal That You Want In A Negotiation: How To Develop The Skill Of Exploring What Is Possible In A Negotiation In Order To Reach The Best Possible Deal

Miscellaneous

- How To Heal A Broken Leg – Fast!: Understanding how to deal with a broken leg in order to start walking again quickly

- How Software Defined Networking (SDN) Is Going To Change Your World Forever: The Revolution In Network Design And How It Affects

Note: See a complete list of books by Dr. Jim Anderson at the back of this book.

Acknowledgements

Any book like this one is the result of years of real-world work experience. In my over 25 years of working for 7 different firms, I have met countless fantastic people and I've been mentored by some truly exceptional ones. Although I've probably forgotten some of the people who made me the person that I am today, here is my attempt to finally give them the recognition that they so truly deserve:

- Thomas P. Anderson
- Art Puett
- Bobbi Marshall
- Bob Boggs

Dr. Jim Anderson

This book is dedicated to my wife Lori. None of this would have been possible without her love and support.

Thanks for the best 24 years of my life (so far)...!

Table Of Contents

THE KEY TO PRODUCT SALES IS GOOD COMMUNICATION 9

ABOUT THE AUTHOR 11

CHAPTER 1: INTERNET PRODUCT PROMOTION – 4 SECRETS FOR PRODUCT MANAGERS 16

CHAPTER 2: PRODUCT LOGO REDESIGN TIME FOR PRODUCT MANGERS 19

CHAPTER 3: TWITTER TOOLS FOR PRODUCT MANAGERS 22

CHAPTER 4: SEXY ADVERTISING: HOW TO GET YOUR PRODUCT NOTICED 26

CHAPTER 5: IS YOUR MARKETING MESSAGE MISSING THE POINT? .. 30

CHAPTER 6: WHY ROI IS THE WRONG WAY TO MEASURE YOUR PRODUCT'S MARKETING PROGRAM 34

CHAPTER 7: THE 6TH PRODUCT MANAGER SENSE: I SEE DEAD PRODUCTS 38

CHAPTER 8: A CHEAP WAY TO STAY IN TOUCH WITH YOUR CUSTOMERS 42

CHAPTER 9: PRODUCT MANAGER: IS IT TIME TO CREATE A CATALOG FOR YOUR PRODUCT? 46

CHAPTER 10: WHAT DOES A PRODUCT MANAGER NEED TO DO AT YOUR NEXT INDUSTRY SHOW? 50

CHAPTER 11: TRADE SHOW SURVIVAL TACTICS FOR PRODUCT MANAGERS 54

CHAPTER 12: 5 SECRETS TO PRODUCT MANGER SUCCESS AT YOUR NEXT TRADE SHOW 59

The Key To Product Sales Is Good Communication

As product managers we know how good our product is. The problem that we are facing is that the rest of the world does not know this. The burden of somehow getting them to know the true value of our product rests on our shoulders – we need to find a way to make this happen. In the end, it all comes down to how good our communication skills are.

In the day and age in which we are living, the internet plays a huge role in how we communicate with our customers. What this means for product managers is that we need to take the time to learn how to leverage this resource to our advantage in order to promote our product. At the same time we can't forget about the power of social media to get the word out about what our product can do.

Before people can buy our product, they have to first notice the product. This can start with the product's logo – does it grab and hold on to the customer's attention? Next we need to take a look at the advertising that we are doing for our product. Is it sexy enough – does it capture our customer's interest and leave them wanting to find out more about the product?

As we spend both time and effort on trying to get the word out about our product, the issue of trying to measure how successful we are being comes up. The traditional way, calculating a return on investment (ROI) does not always match what we are doing. What we need is a better way to capture the value of a product manager's communication efforts.

The secret to good communications between a product manager and their customers is to provide the customer with the information that they want in the format that they want it in. What this means for the product manager is that they are going to have to create several different channels that can be used reach out to customers.

For more information on what it takes to be a great product manager, check out my blog, The Accidental Product Manager, at:

www.TheAccidentalPM.com

Good luck!

- Dr. Jim Anderson

About The Author

I must confess that I never set out to be a product manager. When I went to school, I studied Computer Science and thought that I'd get a nice job programming and that would be that. Well, at least part of that plan worked out!

My first job was working for Boeing on their F/A-18 fighter jet program. I spent my days programming fighter jet software in assembly language and I loved it. The U.S. government decided to save some money and went looking for other countries to sell this plane to. This put me into an unfamiliar role: I started to meet with foreign military officials in order to explain what my product did.

Time moved on and so did I. I found myself working for Siemens, the big German telecommunications company. They were making phone switches and selling them to the seven U.S. phone companies. The problem was that the switches were too complicated. Customers couldn't tell the difference between one complicated phone switch from another complicated phone switch.

The Siemens sales folks were in a bind. They didn't know enough about how the switches worked to tell their customers why they should buy them. Siemens reached out into their engineering unit looking for anyone who could help the sales teams out. I put my hand up and overnight I became a product manager.

Since then I've spent over 20 years working as a product manager for both big companies and startups. This has given me an opportunity to do everything that a product manager does many, many times. I know what works as well as what doesn't work.

I now live in Tampa Florida where I spend my time managing my consulting business, Blue Elephant Consulting, teaching college courses at the University of South Florida, and traveling to work with companies like yours to share the knowledge that I have about how product managers can make their product be a success.

I'm always available to answer questions and I can be reached at:

Dr. Jim Anderson
Blue Elephant Consulting
Email: jim@BlueElephantConsulting.com
Facebook: http://goo.gl/1TVoK
Web: **www.BlueElephantConsulting.com**

"Unforgettable communication skills that will set your ideas free..."

Create Products Your Customers Want At A Price That They Are Willing To Pay!

Dr. Jim Anderson is available to provide training and coaching on the two topics that are the most important to product managers everywhere: how do I create the products that my customers want and what should I price them at?

Dr. Anderson believes that in order to both learn and remember what he says, product managers need to laugh. Each one of his speeches is full of fun and humor so that what he says "sticks" with everyone.

Dr. Anderson's Product Management Training Includes:

1. How can you segment your market?
2. What problems are your customers having right now?
3. Which of your customer's problems does your product solve?
4. How much of this problem does your product solve?
5. How much will it cost your customer if they don't fix this problem?

Dr. Jim Anderson presents over 100 speeches per year. To invite Dr. Anderson to speak at your event, contact him at:

Phone: 813-418-6970 or
Email: jim@BlueElephantConsulting.com

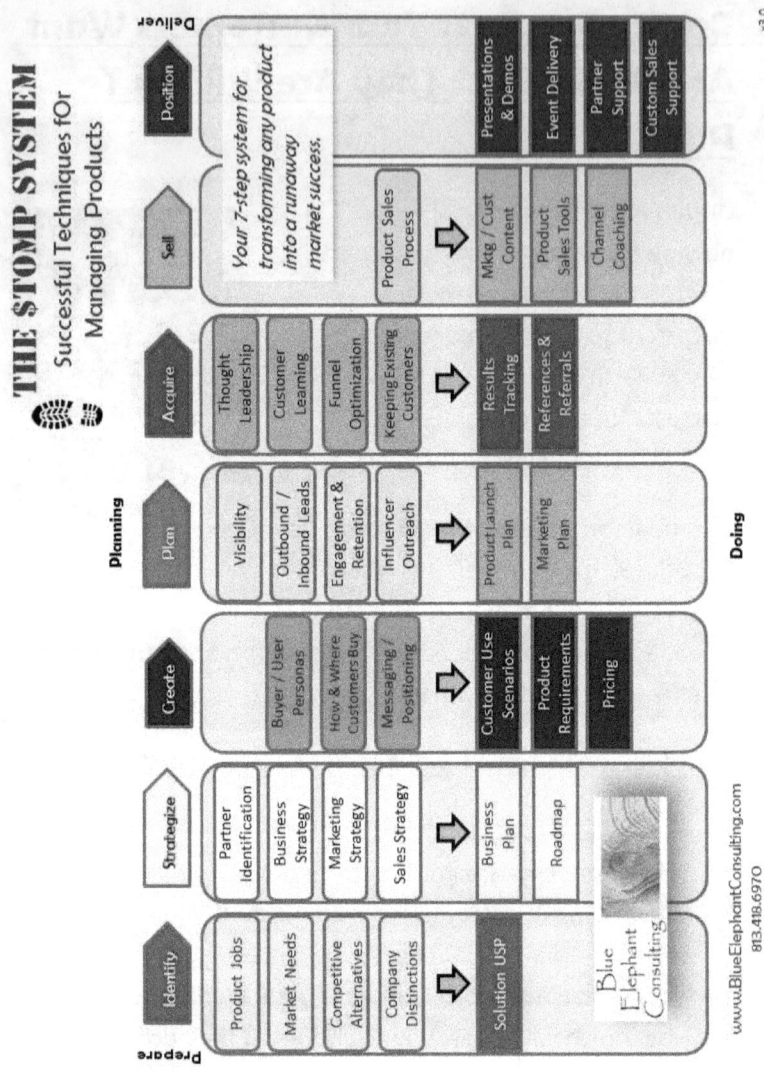

The **$TOMP** product management system has been created by **Blue Elephant Consulting** to help product managers know what to do and when to do it in order for a product to be successful.

Chapter 1

Internet Product Promotion – 4 Secrets For Product Managers

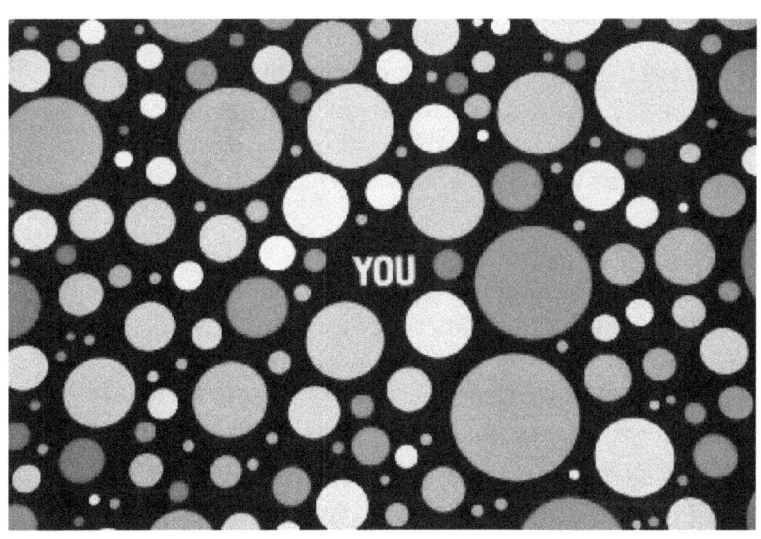

Chapter 1: Internet Product Promotion – 4 Secrets For Product Managers

So there you stand: somehow you've managed to convince the powers that be that your product needs to have its very own web site (or an upgrade to the one that it already has) in order to attract the masses of customers who would be buying it today if only they knew that it existed. Where to start: embedded flash? Viral videos? There's just too many choices! Here's a wake-up call for you – your site's success depends on **four non-technical secrets**.

Kodak Got It Right

Kodak got it right when they talked about people wanting to create a "**Kodak Moment**" – in other words, a memorable experience. Marc Levitt from the MSLK graphic design firm knows a thing or two about creating product web sites that work. He says that your customers need to be rewarded with something new every time they visit or click on something on your product's web site.

This means that you need to spend some time planning what your **customer's experience** on your product's site is going to be. What's the first thing that they will see? How will they navigate? Do you have great and informative content?

Call Now – Operators Are Standing By!

As with so many other things in life, the key to the ultimate success of your product's web site lies in how you go about **promoting it**. Just turning up a new web site and hoping that the rest of the world finds it is not going to cut it. You are going to have to create a marketing plan that will drive people to your new web site. Argh – even more work for the product manager!

Join The Search Patrol

Search has two parts to it that you need to consider: **internal and external**. Internally, you need to have an easy-to-use way for your visitors to search your web site in order to find exactly what they are looking for. Externally you need to design your product's web site in such a way as to maximize its Search Engine Optimization (SEO).

Bring In The Pros

In every company there is somebody that is a wiz at setting up web sites. There may also be a PhotoShop master on board. However, because having a high quality web site for your product requires such a mix of technical, artistic, and marketing skills, this might be one time that you should reach out and **bring in a pro**.

Don't think that you can just open the yellow pages (do those still exist?) and find the perfect firm for you. Instead, you'll have to reach out to **several design firms** and have a talk with them. Review the sites that they've created in the past and determine which firm will do the best job for your product.

Final Thoughts

There is no doubt that the Internet can play a key part in the **success** of any product. How you tell the world about your product on the web is almost as important as how you tell people about it face-to-face.

Taking the time to get the **non-technical** parts of your web site correct is just as important as picking and using the right web technologies. Do this right and you'll make your product fantastically successful.

Chapter 2

Product Logo Redesign Time For Product Mangers

Chapter 2: Product Logo Redesign Time For Product Mangers

So I'm going to guess that you are pretty comfortable with your product by now. You know what it does, you know what it doesn't do. You feel that you've got a pretty good grasp of how your customers view your product. Maybe that's a problem. Is it time for you to **shake things up a bit** and redesign your product's logo?

About That Logo

Not every product has a logo; however, they all should. If you are lucky enough to be in charge of a product that has a logo (or will be someday), then you'll have to redesign the logo sometime. The most common time that logo changes are considered is when a product's name is changed. However, even if this is not the case, then the question that you've got to be asking yourself is "**is this logo working for me?**" If your logo has lost its appeal and is no longer being noticed by your customers, then perhaps it's time to consider a change.

What Needs To Go?

Every logo redesign needs to reflect the current times. Bill Marsh over at the New York Times has looked into what other companies are doing and he's got some tips for product mangers everywhere. In these tough times, companies that have company or product names that are all UPPER CASE are redesigning their logo to include **lower case letters** in order to come across as being more friendly.

Walmart & Kraft Have Redesigned Their Logos To Appear More Friendly

Extras That Help A New Logo

As with everything in life, just changing letters to lower case isn't enough these days. You still have to pick your **colors**. John Bredenfoerder is a color expert and he says that colors that communicate joy and happiness are "in" right now – what better way to uplift people during hard economic times?

Additionally, companies have all flocked to the color **green** in order to communicate how "eco-friendly" their products are, no matter what the product is! Additional **current color favorites** include electric blue, school bus yellow, and of course, red, purple, orange and green.

Final Thoughts

A logo is **not going to sell** your product. Instead, your product's features, your customer service, and the price will be what makes up your customer's mind. However, while the customer is shopping around, a well-designed logo can be the thing that **sticks in their mind** and causes them to come back to your product for another look. Perhaps a logo redesign is just what you need in order to make your product fantastically successful…!

Chapter 3

Twitter Tools For Product Managers

Chapter 3: Twitter Tools For Product Managers

Sigh, ok – I guess that it's time that I finally get around to talking about the Internet fad-du-jour: Twitter. The Internet is all abuzz about just what the heck Twitter is (a micro-blogging service), who should be using it (apparently everyone), and just how product mangers should get the most out of it (a tad bit unclear here). I've spent some time looking into these questions and I think that I've **discovered the answers** that you need.

Some Background On Twitter

So here's the thing: Twitter is not the best thing since sliced bread like some people would have you think. Instead, it's better to view it as being just **another communications tool** that you have at your disposal. One thing that all product managers need to realize is that not everyone is on/using Twitter. This means that this channel is only suited to reaching certain people.

It's Not All About You

Right up front product managers need to realize that other Tweets (people who use Twitter) don't really care about you – instead what they really care about is **your product**. This means that independent of what you may be doing personally on Twitter, you'll need to set up a separate Twitter account for your product. Since Twitter accounts are free, this is easy to do.

Tools For Tracking Tweets

One of the key questions that every product manager wants an answer to is "who is talking about my product?". A great 3rd party tool that let's you do this is called TweetBeep.

With TweetBeep, you sign up for a free account and then you enter the words or phrases that you would like **to keep track of**. TweetBeep will send you an update every hour telling you who has tweeted using the phrase that you are interested in (your product name for example).

Track Re-Tweets

In the world of Twitter, as in the real world, there is very little new. What this means for product managers is that tweets that contain a link often get **re-tweeted multiple times**. In order to find out just how many people are clicking on a link that you tweet about, the company bit.ly offers a service to do this.

Sharp-eyed readers may recognize bit.ly as an online service that you can use to create shorter versions of long URLs. It turns out that bit.ly offers another free service that allows you to attach a **brief code** to your shortened links which will then allow you to **track how many people click on the link** and gather information on them such as where they are located.

Too Many Cooks In The Kitchen

Often when a product manager sets up a single Twitter account for his / her product, there will be **multiple people** within the company who will be responsible for using it and replying to other Tweets. This can quickly become confusing.

A service called CoTweet allows you to set up **multiple queues** for different users. When Tweets about your product are seen, then these tweets can be assigned to different queues so that different users can respond to them. This will help in preventing multiple overlapping responses.

Final Thoughts

Only time will tell if Twitter is here to stay or if it is just a flash-in-the-pan. No matter which way things end up going, product managers have a unique opportunity to use this **new communications channel** to reach out to others and talk about their products.

The basic Twitter service is ok. The arrival of additional 3rd party Twitter tools has the ability to make Twitter an **even more powerful tool** for product mangers. If you learn how to use Twitter effectively, then you will have once again have found out how great product managers make their product(s) **fantastically successful**.

Chapter 4

Sexy Advertising: How To Get Your Product Noticed

Chapter 4: Sexy Advertising: How To Get Your Product Noticed

Just how many ads for products do you get hit with each day? 10? 100? 500? No matter what the number is, the end result is the same – **you shut down**. Something in your brain switches off and you stop "seeing" ads because you are in overload.

This is bad news for a product manager who wants to get his / her product noticed. Is there anything that can be done to get your customers to **notice** your product's advertising?

What Doesn't Work?

You are the CEO for your product and so you're going to have to find a solution to this problem.Ã,Â Dr. Sridhar Balasubramanian and Dr. Pradeep Bhardwaj are marketing professors at the University of North Carolina's Kenan-Flagler Business School and they've been studying this problem of how to reach customers that have **tuned traditional product advertising out**.

The professors point out that most product managers take the aggressive approach and attempt to get their products noticed by simply **TALKING LOUDER** (remember those TV ads with "Crazy Larry"?) This simply doesn't work.

Questions That You Need To Be Asking

There are 5 things that as a product manager you can do in order to ensure that the advertising for your product is actually working for you. Here's what you need to be doing today in order to get your product noticed tomorrow:

Pick The Right Time: You know your (potential) customers better than anyone else. When will they NOT be getting hit with too many ads – when they get their postal mail at work? Via Twitter? Via FedEx box? Find your customer's quiet time and seize it to get your message across. **Examples:** the in-flight magazine that everyone reads is a great opportunity to reach the right type of customer when they are "locked in" and have nothing else to read, also those adding your product to those videos that they are starting to show in elevators would be a great way to reach your target customers in their building.

Arouse Curiosity: Ads that just talk about how great a product is are boring. Ads that trigger your customer's curiosity are something special. Is there a puzzle that you can create that they have to solve? Once they solve it can they go to your product's web site and claim a reward? Talk about a great way to get your message across! **Example:** Google did this when they were hiring – they created billboards with math problems and a URL where you could go to type in the answer.

Piggyback On Another Brand: If your product is new, you are going to be fighting for your potential customer's attention because they don't know anything about your product. However, if you can join forces with an existing brand, then both brands can benefit from combined advertising. **Example:** you see this all the time – summer movies do cross promotions with McDonald's and Burger King,

Physically Move Into Your Customer's World: Where does your customer spend most of their day? In days of old, companies sent out calendars to their potential customers (Pirelli's is world famous) because they knew that they would be on the wall for a year. **Example:** Today providing your customers with a browser widget might be the best way to promote your product.

Trigger All 5 Human Senses: Ok, so maybe you can't hit all five senses but can you at least do one better than sight? A clever tune or a pleasant scent that becomes associated with your product could help it stand out from all of the other ads that your customer encounters. **Example:** The Coke "jingle" and the Southwest "ding" sound are both audible sounds that we all now associate with the brands. If we hear the sounds, then we automatically think of the brand!

Final Thoughts

As though being a product manager was not hard enough, now we have to be advertising experts? Well, no. However, you are the one person who is **ultimately responsible** for the success of your product. You need to be asking these 5 questions so that you can steer the advertising for your product so that in the end, it works to make your product **fantastically successful**.

Product managers who find ways to use advertising to make their products even sexier to their customers will have found yet another way that great product managers make their product(s) **fantastically successful**.

Chapter 5

Is Your Marketing Message Missing
The Point?

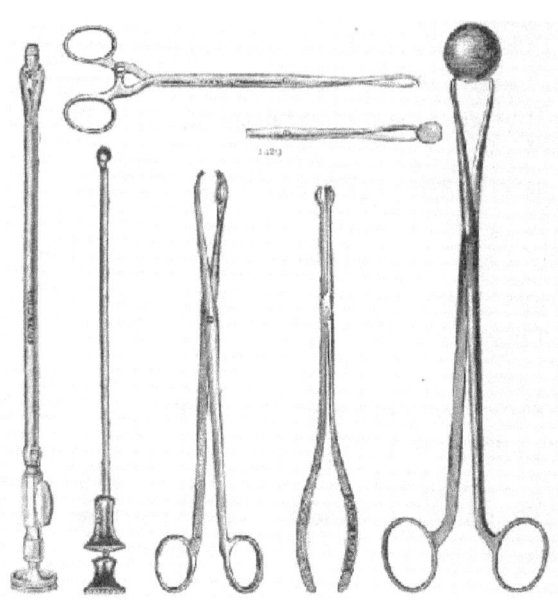

Chapter 5: Is Your Marketing Message Missing The Point?

If you were going fishing, how much luck catching fish do you think that you would have **if you didn't use any bait on your hook**? Sure, there are probably some either dumb or near-sighted fish that might still bite, but you're going to be doing a lot of sitting around waiting. Is it possible that as a product manager you are fishing for customers for your product without bait?

The Problem With Market Assumptions

As a product manager you work hard to create a product that meets what you think the **needs of your customers are**. Once you've got the product ready to go to market, you whip up some sales brochures that are loaded with your marketing message, create a slide presentation or two, and then dump them on your sales teams and tell them to go sell, sell, sell!

Now this is all find and good if you've guessed right. Or maybe a better way for me to have said that was it's all good if you've correctly guessed what your customer's needs are. If you haven't, then you're sending your sales teams off to fish **without any bait.**

Your market assumptions are those points that you build your marketing message around. Market assumptions are the **reasons** that you believe that your customers will be willing to purchase your product. If you get this wrong, then nothing else matters.

An Example Of Marketing Mis-Alignment

These types of things are always most clearly understood when there is a good example. In this case, the writer Geoffrey James has uncovered the case of the product managers at Ascent Healthcare Solutions getting their marketing message misaligned.

Ascent takes used medical devices (catheters, drill bits, bags, etc.), cleans, sterilizes, and tests them before selling them back to hospitals for about **half of their original price.**

The product managers at Ascent thought that they understood their customer very well – price conscious hospitals. Their marketing assumption was that if they convinced their customers that reprocessed products were **safe**, then they would buy them. It turns out that they were wrong.

When sales didn't take off like they were supposed to, Ascent brought in consultants to sit down with Ascent's customers and find out what was really going on. It turns out that hospitals were already convinced that Ascent's products were safe to use. The problem was that Ascent's product managers had assumed that **switching over** to collecting and tuning in medical devices to be reconditioned was an easy thing to do. Hospitals didn't see it that way.

Just like every large organization, **any sort of change is always a real pain**. Hospitals saw the need to set up special recycling bags just for the devices that Ascent could recondition and then teaching the hospital staff new procedures to use was going to be more hassle than the savings were worth.

Once Ascent learned about their marketing mistake, they quickly corrected their message out to the market. They no longer assume that hospitals will view reprocessing as being easy, they have changed their marketing message to now state that **"Ascent makes reprocessing easy."**

What All Of This Means For You

Right now you are operating under a set of marketing assumptions about your customers. You might be right or you might be wrong. If your assumptions are incorrect, then you could be **missing out** on a lot of customers.

The first step is for you to write down just exactly what your current marketing messages are. You are probably going to need **an outsider** to help you do this because you may be too close to your material to be able to "see" your messages.

Next, you are going to have to **test your messages**. This is going to require you to work with the sales team and start to have discussions with customers. This includes not only existing customers, but ones who have left you. Ask them if what you think are their most pressing needs really are driving their decisions.

I speak from experience when I tell you that you are probably in for some **surprises**. All too often, just like the product managers at Ascent, we can start to believe our own marketing material and that's how we can get out of alignment with our customers.

Chapter 6

Why ROI Is The WRONG Way To Measure Your Product's Marketing Program

Chapter 6: Why ROI Is The WRONG Way To Measure Your Product's Marketing Program

Ah the world of product marketing — it's where artists dream up brightly colored logos and put together viral YouTube videos that nobody really understands but everyone has to watch and send to their friends. Well, as a product manager you may think that that is what goes on in the world of marketing, but in the end you really don't care. What you want is **results**, in other words more sales of your product. Let's reign in the magic unicorns that live in marketing and try to come up with a way to measure what we're getting for what we're spending. Maybe ROI is the way to go...

Everything Is Easier On The Web

Surprise, surprise! In the past few years everyone has fallen in love with marketing / pushing their products on the web. Forget newspapers, magazines, radio, and TV — the web is where it's at. One of the big reasons that everyone's in love with the web (besides the fact that it's all new and shiny) is that it seems to offer **a fantastic return on investment (ROI)** .

In a nutshell, what everyone believes is that when you use the web to reach out and contact your customers and potential customers, it costs you **next to nothing**. In turn, if anyone happens to buy your product because you got in touch with them over the web then ta-da you've just "found" money.

The problem with all of this comes when we start to take a closer look at just what we really mean by getting "**results**" from a web-only based campaign. If we dumb things down and just use some measure of ROI as a way to gauge how we are doing, we may be missing some important information.

It's All About Relationships

How about if we take a collective step back here for just a minute. Whenever you do marketing for your product, what's your goal? Deep down what are you really trying to accomplish? The real role of marketing is to **generate leads** which is just a fancy term for "find people who have a problem that might be solved by your product".

Just telling people about your product once is often not enough. In many cases you actually have to **change people's behavior** before they will become a lead for your product. Getting people to change their behaviors and become a lead is what the real objective of your marketing efforts are. How well you are meeting these objectives is what you really need to be measuring. Maybe calling it "return on objective" (ROO) is what we should be doing.

An Example Of An ROO

David Shoenfeld is a VP at the U.S. Postal Service and he knows a thing or two about balancing web marketing with other channels. As an example of an ROO for product marketing he talks about the product managers who worked for **a hospital in Kentucky**.

Hospital product managers, you say? Why not — a hospital is actually a collection of **very specialized products** that get sold to customers and so product managers are needed to play a key role in managing and marketing those products.

This particular hospital wanted to get **more referrals** from doctors ("go have your surgery at this hospital") because there's a lot of money in them thar referrals. The product managers initially did what we all would do right off the bat: they sent out an email blast to all of the local doctors asking for more referrals. Nothing happened.

A little research revealed the flaw in their plan: in order to get more doctors to refer their patients to the hospital really required a **deeper relationship** between the doctor — hospital — patient. This meant that to get the results that they were looking for the product managers had to roll out a multi-channel marketing campaign. This included direct mail, TV ads, and even sponsoring some health lectures in the community.

What All Of This Means For You

I know that you've heard this before, but in my opinion you just can't hear it enough: before you start any marketing program for your product, you need to make sure that you are very clear on **the objectives** of what you are hoping to accomplish.

Yes, money is important. However, since what you really want to do is to **determine how well you are meeting your objectives**, you need to be able to look beyond the dollars and see how you are doing on meeting your overall objectives.

Make sure that when you invest the time, money, and energy into your next marketing program for your product, you do it right and **actually connect with your intended customers**. Do this well, and your product can't help but be successful.

Chapter 7

The 6th Product Manager Sense: I See Dead Products

Chapter 7: The 6th Product Manager Sense: I See Dead Products

Does the recession have you down? How's your product doing — nobody buying, nobody interested? Cheer up — it turns out that this is actually **the best time to be a product manager**. Recessions are some of the best times for product managers to create new products that shake up the market and make your existing customers want you even more. The secret is to realize that what you have to do is to challenge convention...

What Does A Product Manager Need To Do To Survive A Recession?

If you decide to hunker down and try to wait out the current recession, then what you are really doing is acting like a blade of grass that doesn't realize that the lawnmower will eventually come around and get it. All product managers know that ideas are cheap. You **don't have to spend a lot of money** to solve problems with your product, instead what you do need to spend is that most precious of all resources: your time.

Dr. Andrew Razeghi is an author, consultant, and teacher at Northwestern's Kellogg School of Management who has written about **how to prosper** in tough times. He has some suggestions for all of us.

He points out that product managers only need **three things** in order to innovate: ideas, talent, and capital. As we are all probably painfully aware of, your company is probably currently totally focused on capital and what they can do to conserve it.

Just so that we're all on the same page here, let us agree that the right thing to be doing is to be mindful of capital spending even as we **stay in front of our customers** so that we can hear what they are telling us. We then need to use this information to make investments in our product that will pay off in the long term.

The Worst Thing That A Product Manager Can Do

Right now the #1 thing that most product managers don't want to do is go out and **be in front of our customers** — why bother, nobody's buying. This is exactly the wrong thing to do. Cutting off communication with your customers is (always) a terrible thing to do.

When your customers and potential customers **stop hearing from you** this causes them to start to wonder. They start to think to themselves "Are these guys still in business?", "Should I buy from them — are they stable?", etc.

The right thing to do now is to find more ways to stay in contact with your customers. Your goal needs to be to do everything that you can to **increase your customer's confidence** not only in your product, but also in the company that stands behind that product.

What Should A Product Manager Be Doing?

Saying that you should be challenging convention is one thing and actually doing it is something else. Forget about **flashy Superbowl ads**, the key thing to remember is that anything that you can do that will save your customers time or make their job easier will always be relevant and interesting to them.

In this age of Internet-everything, one possible way for a product manager to make his / her product more relevant to their customers is to engage in some **sensory branding** with your customers. This sounds all new-agey, but it's really a very old concept.

Product marketing that is done over the Internet can only really appeal to one of your customer's senses: sight. That leaves **four others** that are not being used. If you can find a way to engage two or more of these senses, then you've got a much better chance of making a lasting connection with your customer.

This could be as simple as postal mailing a letter to your customer that is printed on heavy parchment paper. It has been shown that people still **trust** what they read on paper more than what they read on a screen. The use of heavy paper will appeal to your customer's sense of touch and will add "weight" to your words.

What All Of This Means For You

It's all too easy to get yourself down during a recession — your sales are slipping and everyone (including your customers) seems to be in a blue funk. Hold on a minute, since when were you ever taught to do **exactly what everyone else is doing?**

Since no product manager ever made their product a success by following the herd, this is exactly the time for you to try different things — **what's the risk?** One simple and effective technique that any product manager can try is to study how they are currently connecting with their customers. The next step is to build on this and find ways to engage more of your customer's senses in order to build their interest in and desire for your product.

These are both the best of times and worst of times. As a successful product manager you need to **take action** to make sure that both you and your product come out of it ahead of the pack.

Chapter 8

A Cheap Way To Stay In Touch With Your Customers

Chapter 8: A Cheap Way To Stay In Touch With Your Customers

So let me guess, the travel budget for your product which was measly to begin with **has been slashed to the bone** and you're going to be home for dinner for the foreseeable future. That's great news if you don't like to travel, but it sorta sucks if you want to stay in contact with your customer, discover their pain points, and uncover new product requirements. What's a product manager to do?

Maybe Email Isn't So Bad After All

I almost hesitate to say this, but have you thought about using more email to stay in touch with both your existing customers and your prospects? Yeah, yeah I know that we all shudder at the though of bombarding our customers with even more email than they are already getting, but in these difficult times **perhaps this is what we need to be doing**.

What innovative product managers are discovering is that some well-done emails are turning out to be quite effective and even, dare I say it, **personal**. It turns out that email is apparently a tool that we use with abandon internally, but it can also be an effective external tool with which to make strong customer connections.

The reason that email seems to work so well has to do with the simple fact that your customers view it as **being non-threatening**. Instead of having to deal with finding the time to have a face-to-face meeting with you and potentially getting bombarded with lots of product questions that they may not have the answers to, they are in the driver's seat. After all, they can always delete your email if they want to...

Product Manager Secrets To Successful Emails

So if email is this secret path to your customer's heart, then why don't we do a better job of using it? I mean we must write like a million of these things every week so **shouldn't we be pretty good at it by now?**

Well, **no actually**, we're not all that good at it.

The first thing that we often overlook is the most important part of any email, its **subject line**. Look, this is the $1,000,000 waterfront property part of your email, why would you waste it? I can't tell you how many emails I get that have either a blank subject line or a single word like "Issue" or "Problem". What a waste!

The purpose of an email's subject is to **motivate me to open it up**. I get so much email every day that if your email looks like its going to be boring, there is a very good chance that I won't open it and that it will end up getting deleted later on when I'm on one of my "clean out the email inbox" rages.

The next mistake that product managers make is that they make their emails **too long**. In other words, they type like they talk. Since you are writing to your customer, you have the ability to go back after you've written the email and edit it long before your customer ever sees it. All too often, we skip this critical step and create these lengthy "War and Peace" length novels that nobody takes the time to actually read.

Finally, all too often our emails are basically junk. We write the email with no real purpose in mind and the resulting email is basically empty blather. What we should be doing is finding **value-adding content** and then using emails to get this critical information into our customer's hands.

What All Of This Means For You

When times get tough, one of the first things that companies often cut back on is the travel budgets that product managers use to get in front of our customers. When this happens, the very worst thing that we can do is sit back and passively start to **lose contact** with our customers.

Instead, what we need to be doing is finding creative new ways to stay **in our customer's minds** even if we can't be physically present. The old standby email is one tool that often gets overlooked.

This can be a dangerous tool — in the wrong hands, email can end up doing more damage to your relationship with your customer than good. However, if you take the time to think out what you want to communicate to your customer and then do it creatively in a brief way then you will have found a way to **connect with** your most valuable asset — your customers.

Chapter 9

Product Manager: Is It Time To Create A Catalog For Your Product?

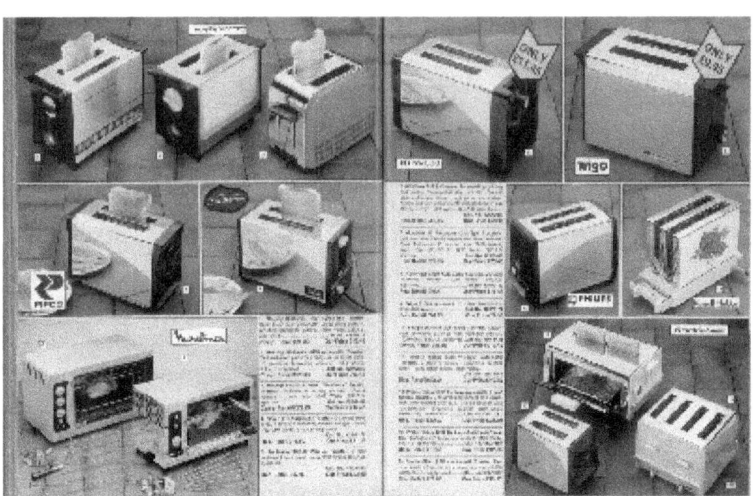

Chapter 9: Product Manager: Is It Time To Create A Catalog For Your Product?

So here's a novel thought for you to consider Product Manager: **why not create a catalog for your product?** Based on a recommendation from a friend, I've been reading the book "Catalog Design: Creating Desire" and it has given me a whole new appreciation for catalogs. I used to just get them in the mail, scan them quickly, and then toss them aside. Now I better understand just what a valuable product tool they are...

Look, no matter if you are a product manager for a single product or for a whole line of products, you are actually selling a number of different things. Whether it's different configurations of your product(s), training, different bundles, different support programs, etc. **we are all selling more than just one thing**. This opens the door to creating a catalog to describe to our customers everything that we sell.

As product managers we are always thinking about our competition. We'd all love to have a way to make our products **stand out in their markets**. Since none of us have an unlimited budget, it's time to get creative. Does any of your competition currently create a catalog for their products? If not, then you've got a real opportunity here.

Brochures don't count. A catalog is a "book" that allows you to lay out everything that you offer to your customers in one place. A brochure just provides information on one product. A catalog will allow you to **build an image** for both your product and your company.

What does it take to make a catalog?

In order to create a catalog, you need to first start by selecting a theme that you want to use for your catalog. This is going to depend greatly on the type of product that you manage and the people who are your customers. Remember, businesses don't buy products, people do. The theme needs to be something that your customers will respond to – **something that they want to be part of**.

Once you have a theme selected, you next need images – photos. You are going to need a lot of these because the whole purpose of a catalog is to allow your customer to **experience your product**. Don't even think about filling a catalog with screenshots of some software product. Instead, spend some time and think about what your customers do with your product and include images of the end results that your customers want to achieve.

Finally, you're going to need words. But not just any words. The words that you drape in and around your photos need to explain what your customer is seeing in the photos and how they can get the same results. The tone and the specific words that you use **need to reinforce the theme that you've chosen**.

How do you go about using a catalog?

Once you've gone to the effort of creating your catalog, the next step is the most important. You're going to have to sit down with your sales team and go through the catalog page by page in order to **make sure that they understand it**.

One they understand the theme, the content, and the intent of the catalog, then they can take it to their customers. As a part of their selling process they can go through the catalog with their customers in order to show them what's in it and to **motivate them to take a closer look** after the salesperson is gone.

Finally, you will also need to update that part of your company's web site that deals with your product. Its look and feel needs to be the same as the theme that you used in the catalog. As customers read the catalog and decide to visit your web site to learn more, **the theme should carry over to the web site.**

What does all of this mean to you?

No matter how fancy we get in this all-electronics age, it turns out that **catalogs still serve a purpose**. They do a fantastic job of laying out in one place a company's entire line of products and telling a story to your customers. Catalogs are not going away anytime soon.

As an example of this I'll refer you to my favorite catalog, Cruchfield. They do a great job of transforming commodity electronics into a product that **you really want to buy from them**.

Catalogs can provide a product manager with a unique way to **make your product stand out in a crowded market**. Please note that creating a catalog is the start of a long-term commitment. Once you've created one, your customers are going to be eager to see the next edition…

Chapter 10

What Does A Product Manager Need To Do At Your Next Industry Show?

Chapter 10: What Does A Product Manager Need To Do At Your Next Industry Show?

As the global economy snaps back, product managers are going to start traveling once again. Where will we be going? One place that we should plan on spending some time will be at **industry trade shows** (pause for collective groan). No, these are not the most enjoyable things to go to just to hand out your business card; however, maybe you feel this way because nobody ever told you how to get the most out a trade show...

It's All About Having Goals

In all of my years of attending countless trade shows, it's only been in the past 10 or so that I've gotten my act together and started **creating goals for what I want to accomplish while I'm there**. As simple as this may sound, there's actually a trick to doing it right.

The goals that you set need to consist of creating a specific business purpose that has an associated objective that is quantifiable. It can be very easy to get caught up in the show (the ton of pre-show material that you get can help to build the hype), but in the end identifying who you want to talk with and what you want to learn **will make sure that your time is well spent**.

Time Management Counts At Trade Shows Also

You wouldn't show up for work without having a plan (would you?) so you need to have a plan in place **BEFORE** you hit a trade show. You can create your plan by taking the time to read the convention promotion material and go over the meeting agendas.

If you want to take it to the next level, you can spend time studying **the layout of the show floor** so that you know what vendor booths you want to visit and in which order you are going to want to visit them. Just before the show, take an hour and surf the web sites of the firms that you are thinking about visiting and make a final decision as to if you want to spend the time with them.

It's All About Appointments

To get the most out of any show, the best way to maximize your time is to **schedule appointments with customers and vendors** before the show. Now you are not the only one to realize this and so you'll have to set up your appointments well before the show date in order to get on everyone's calendar.

Too Much Really Is Too Much

A trade show is a dynamic event – you might think that you know what is going to happen before the show, **but things can change either before or during show**. This means that you don't want to fully book your day – leave open times. This "free time" will become valuable as you meet new people at the show and want to have discussions with them.

Having a list of **back-up people and booths that you'd be willing to visit with** is always a good idea. If an appointment cancels on you or if a scheduled vendor doesn't show up, you'll need to have a plan to fill in your sudden free time.

Work With Non-Competing Firms

Look, any trade show is probably too much for you to handle as a lone product manager. Even if other people from your company are going, you could still **quickly end up being**

overloaded. One way to deal with this situation is to enlist help from product managers at other firms.

This might sound a little weird to you, but here's how it goes. You reach out to your network of product managers who work for other non-competing companies and find out who will be attending the same show. You call them up and find out what they are going to be pushing at the show. Likewise, you tell them what you'll be promoting. Finally, you offer to send any prospects that you run into their way if they'll do the same for you. This can be a great way to reach out to potential customers that **you might not otherwise be able to contact**.

What All Of This Means For You

A trade show can easily appear to be a big waste of time – if a product manager is not prepared in advance for it. However, if you take the time to plan out what you'll be doing, it can turn into a **big success** for both you and your product.

The key is to **take the time before the show** to sit down and identify what you really want to accomplish, who you want to meet with, and how you can get your message out to the most people who will be at the show.

Time is the one thing that product managers never seem to have enough of. Trade shows can be an enormous waste of time if you don't plan for them. However, by doing some planning before the big show, you can transform this potential waste of time into **a big boost for your career and your product**.

Chapter 11

Trade Show Survival Tactics For Product Managers

Chapter 11: Trade Show Survival Tactics For Product Managers

by drjim on March 22, 2010[edit]

Don't Just Stand Around At Your Next Trade Show, Do Some Learning!

I can only speak for myself, but I actually enjoy going to industry trade shows. It's time out of the office, I get to hang out with other people who work in my industry who can feel my pain (whatever it happens to be this year), and I get to see a bunch of friends that seem to rotate between companies every couple of years. That being said, the reason that I get to go to a trade show is because I'm expected to do things there that will **help my product be more successful**. That is the part that requires some preparation on my part...

Bring Your Utility Belt

A trade show is a constant swirl of people – almost too many to keep track of. You'll be bumping into people all the time and so you need to be ready to **make the most of every encounter**.

At the very least, you're going to need to be able to quickly tell people that you meet about your product. Since you'll just have a brief amount of time to do this, you need to have one of those **30-second "elevator speeches"** ready and waiting.

I can speak from experience when I tell you that you can meet somebody one minute and then forget their name the next. That's why having a huge stack of business cards is a requirement. Your goal is not to hold on to these, instead **give them out like they were water**.

Look Out For Changes

When it comes to trade shows, nothing is set in stone. This means that how you thought you were going to spend your time **may not turn out to be how it goes**.

The schedule of presentations and demonstrations that you wanted to attend & see at the show are the first thing that can change. Upon arriving at the show, take a moment to pick up a **revised version of the show's agenda**. A quick scan should let you know if you've got some re-planning to do.

Meetings that you may have set up with clients or vendors can also change. It's not unusual for people's travel plans to change due to work or family issues. If you've had someone cancel on you, the start of the show is the time to realize it **so that you can work to fill the gap**.

Rub Shoulders With Customers

When a product manager goes to a trade show, it's all too easy to think like a product manger while you are there. Instead, what you want to be doing is spending your time **thinking like one of your customers**. Where would they spend their time?

If you take a look at the presentations that will be given during the show, often times there will some that are targeted towards vendors (that's you) and some that are targeted towards customers. As enticing as the vendor material might be, you really should be spending your time going to the presentations that will give you a chance to **mix and mingle with potential customers**. This will give you the biggest bang for your buck.

Talk To The Old Hands

Every show has a particular personality. If you can find someone who has been to the show in the past, they can be a great source of information on what to do while you are there – **and what not to waste your time on**.

What you are really going to want to learn is **what your customers and vendors will be doing while they are there**. Get information on the best hotels to stay at, when people actually show up, and what social events are worth your time.

Take A Team Approach

One product manager can only accomplish so much at a trade show. Instead of trying to do it all yourself, **work with the other folks from your company who will be going**.

The key to making the most of a group is to **come up with a plan** before going. Dividing up responsibilities based on areas of interest or specific groups of vendors or customers is often the best bet.

In order to make the most of doing this, you'll need to make sure that the group **has a huddle** once you get back to the office in order to compare notes.

What All Of This Means For You

A trade show can be a very efficient way for a product manager to get a lot of marketing activities accomplished in a short amount of time. The key to making the most of your time is to **come prepared**.

Having a quick & clear story about your product along with lots of business cards is a great way to start. Staying on top of changes in the show's schedule and people's schedules **is necessary in order to make the most of your time**.

Spending time talking to people who have gone to the show in the past can point you in the right direction. **Make the most of your time and you can get more out of the show then just a bunch of brochures…**

Chapter 12

5 Secrets To Product Manger Success At Your Next Trade Show

Chapter 12: 5 Secrets To Product Manger Success At Your Next Trade Show

Think back over all of that university training that you (or your parents) paid for. Just for a good measure, throw in all of that training that you've sat through since you started working. Wow – that's a lot of learning. One quick question for you: in all of that classroom / online time, **did anyone ever take the time to tell you how to "do" a tradeshow correctly?** Did they ever sit you down and explain to you how a product manager can get the most out of each trade show experience? Hmm, looks like there is a gap in your education – let's see if we can fill you in...

Email Is Bad!

Picture the scene: you're at a trade show and you've just sat through a great presentation on the challenges that your customers will be facing during the upcoming year. The session is over, everyone piles out of the doors and then what happens? More often than not, **standing alone, everyone whips out their Blackberry's / iPhones and starts to check and answer emails**. What a waste!

Look, being at a tradeshow is a unique opportunity for you as a product manager to rub shoulders with all sorts of people who may be important to the success of both you and your product. Don't waste your time doing email while you are at the show, **email will wait** and you can do it later on.

Mom Was Wrong: You Should Talk To Strangers

Depending how many times you've been to a given show, there are probably a number of people that you already know who will be there. Don't waste your time talking to them (do talk to them, but not too much). Instead, **go talk to strangers**.

You can always get in touch with people that you already have a relationship with – they know you and you know how to get in touch with them. While at the show, spend your valuable time **reaching out to people that you don't already know** (and giving away your business cards). A tradeshow is a once-a-year opportunity to quickly create new relationships that may benefit both you and your product.

No Sleep 'Til Brooklyn

Let's be honest about this, we're all getting older. No matter how sharp you think that your brain is, so much happens each day at a trade show that if you don't take some time at the end of the day to sort things out, then **you'll forget too much**.

You need to keep in mind that you don't need to wait until the trade show is over before **you start to use what you've learned**. Use the end of each day to sort out the information that you've collected, send emails to others and yourself with instructions based on information learned, and generally use what you've learned one day to prepare for the next day.

Can We Do A Trade Show?

With travel budgets being cut to the bone and you having less and less available time to get things done, trade shows can be a godsend. Specifically, they are a great time to meet up with all of those people that **you should have been talking with, but haven't been**.

To make the most of the event, don't just leave things to chance. Instead, make calls and send emails to vendors and partners a week before the show and **schedule time to meet up with them and have a quick talk**. This will make up for the visits that you should have made earlier in the year.

Follow Up, Follow Up, Follow Up

You would think that after having invested all of that time in preparing for and then attending a trade show, product managers would do a good job of following up after the show. **You would be wrong**.

All too often we put everything that we collected into that bag that they gave us at the show and then we come home, tuck the bag with its brochures, badge holder, and collected business cards away somewhere and **promptly forget about it**. Instead, you need to create a clear plan for what you want to do with the new information that you've collected and the contacts that you've made. Oh, and don't forget to send out thank-you's to people that you've met for the first time.

What All Of This Means For You

Trade shows can **take up a great deal of your time**. On top of everything else that you need to be doing, this can end up putting you even farther behind in what you need to be accomplishing if you aren't careful.

However, if you prepare to get the most out of a trade show, then it can be **time well spent**. Using it to make new contacts and collect needed new information can turn a required use of your time into a desired used of time.

Use the suggestions that we've covered when you attend your next industry trade show. **The results will speak for themselves**...

It's from the forge of failure that the steel of success is formed.

Hard Work Does Not Guarantee Success, But Success Does Not Happen Without Hard Work.

- Dr. Jim Anderson

Create Products Your Customers Want At A Price That They Are Willing To Pay!

Dr. Jim Anderson is available to provide training and coaching on the two topics that are the most important to product managers everywhere: how do I create the products that my customers want and what should I price them at?

Dr. Anderson believes that in order to both learn and remember what he says, product managers need to laugh. Each one of his speeches is full of fun and humor so that what he says "sticks" with everyone.

Dr. Anderson's Product Management Training Includes:

1. How can you segment your market?
2. What problems are your customers having right now?
3. Which of your customer's problems does your product solve?
4. How much of this problem does your product solve?
5. How much will it cost your customer if they don't fix this problem?

Dr. Jim Anderson presents over 100 speeches per year. To invite Dr. Anderson to speak at your event, contact him at:

Phone: 813-418-6970 or
Email: jim@BlueElephantConsulting.com

Blue Elephant Consulting
Speaking   Negotiating   Managing   Markets

Photo Credits:

Cover – Anne Worner
https://www.flickr.com/photos/wefi_official/

Chapter 1 - Gisela Giardino
https://www.flickr.com/photos/gi/

Chapter 2 - SimonQ錫濛譙🄯
https://www.flickr.com/photos/qiaomeng/

Chapter 3 - Andrea Incalza
https://www.flickr.com/photos/cetaceo/

Chapter 4 – Dr. Jim Anderson

Chapter 5 - Arallyn!
https://www.flickr.com/photos/biomedical_scraps/

Chapter 6 - Reymond Galvez
https://www.flickr.com/photos/reymondgalvez/

Chapter 7 – Rotten Tomatoes
https://www.rottentomatoes.com/m/sixth_sense/

Chapter 8 - Caleb Roenigk
https://www.flickr.com/photos/crdot/

Chapter 9 – mattbeee
https://www.flickr.com/photos/querth/

Chapter 10 - IAVM WHQ
https://www.flickr.com/photos/iavmwhq/

Chapter 11 - IAVM WHQ
https://www.flickr.com/photos/iavmwhq/

Chapter 12 - IAVM WHQ
https://www.flickr.com/photos/iavmwhq/

Other Books By The Author

Product Management

- How Product Managers Can Sell More Of Their Product: Tips & Techniques For Product Managers To Better Understand How To Sell Their Product

- How Product Managers Can Sell More Of Their Product: Tips & Techniques For Product Managers To Better Understand How To Sell Their Product

- How To Create A Successful Product That Customers Will Want: Techniques For Product Managers To Boost Product Sales And Increase Customer Satisfaction

- What Product Managers Need To Know About World-Class Product Development: How Product Managers Can Create Successful Products

- How Product Managers Can Learn To Understand Their Customers: Techniques For Product Managers To Better Understand What Their Customers Really Want

- Product Management Secrets: Techniques For Product Managers To Boost Produ Michael Kct Sales And Increase Customer Satisfaction

- Product Development Lessons For Product Managers: How Product Managers Can Create Successful Products

- Customer Lessons For Product Managers: Techniques For Product Managers To Better Understand What Their Customers Really Want

- Product Failure Lessons For Product Managers: Examples Of Products That Have Failed For Product Managers To Learn From

- Communication Skills For Product Managers: The Communication Skills That Product Managers Need To Know How To Use In Order To Have A Successful Product

- How To Have A Successful Product Manager Career: The Things That You Need To Be Doing TODAY In Order To Have A Successful Product Manager Career

- Product Manager Product Success: How to keep your product on track and make it become a success

Public Speaking

- How To Organize A Speech In Order To Make Your Point: How to put together a speech that will capture and hold your audience's attention

- Changing How You Speak To Overcome Your Fear Of Speaking: Change techniques that will transform a speech into a memorable event

- Delivering Excellence: How To Give Presentations That Make A Difference: Presentation techniques that will transform a speech into a memorable event

- Tools Speakers Need In Order To Give The Perfect Speech: What tools to use to create your next speech so that your message will be remembered forever!

- How To Create A Speech That Will Be Remembered

- Secrets To Organizing A Speech For Maximum Impact: How to put together a speech that will capture and hold your audience's attention

- How To Become A Better Speaker By Changing How You Speak: Change techniques that will transform a speech into a memorable event

- How To Give A Great Presentation: Presentation techniques that will transform a speech into a memorable event

- How To Rehearse In Order To Give The Perfect Speech: How to effectively rehearse your next speech to that your message be remembered forever!

- Secrets To Creating The Perfect Speech: How to create a speech that will make your message be remembered forever!

- Secrets To Organizing The Perfect Speech: How to organize the best speech of your life!

- Secrets To Planning The Perfect Speech: How to plan to give the best speech of your life

- How To Show What You Mean During A Presentation: How to use visual techniques to transform a speech into a memorable event

CIO Skills

- New IT Technology Issues Facing CIOs: How CIOs Can Stay On Top Of The Changes In The Technology That Powers The Company

- Keeping The Barbarians Out: How CIOs Can Secure Their Department and Company: Tips And Techniques For CIOs To Use In Order To Secure Both Their IT Department And Their Company

- What CIOs Need To Know In Order To Successfully Manage An IT Department: Decision Making Skills That Every CIO Needs To Have In Order To Be Able To Make The Right Choices

- Becoming A Powerful And Effective Leader: Tips And Techniques That IT Managers Can Use In Order To Develop Leadership Skills

- CIO Secrets For Growing Innovation: Tips And Techniques For CIOs To Use In Order To Make Innovation Happen In Their IT Department

- Your Success As A CIO Depends On How Well You Communicate: Tips And Techniques For CIOs To Use In Order To Become Better Communicators

- What CIOs Need To Know About Working With Partners: Techniques For CIOs To Use In Order To Be Able To Successfully Work With Partners

- Critical CIO Management Skills: Decision Making Skills That Every CIO Needs To Have In Order To Be Able To Make The Right Choices

- How CIOs Can Make Innovation Happen: Tips And Techniques For CIOs To Use In Order To Make Innovation Happen In Their IT Department

- CIO Communication Skills Secrets: Tips And Techniques For CIOs To Use In Order To Become Better Communicators

- Managing Your CIO Career: Steps That CIOs Have To Take In Order To Have A Long And Successful Career

- CIO Business Skills: How CIOs can work effectively with the rest of the company!

IT Manager Skills

- How IT Managers Can Use New Technology To Meet Today's IT Challenges: Technologies That IT Managers Can Use In Order to Make Their Teams More Productive

- How To Build High Performance IT Teams: Tips And Techniques That IT Managers Can Use In Order To Develop Productive Teams

- Save Yourself, Save Your Job – How To Manage Your IT Career: Secrets That IT Managers Can Use

In Order To Have A Successful Career

- Growing Your CIO Career: How CIOs Can Work With The Entire Company In Order To Be Successful

- How IT Managers Can Make Innovation Happen: Tips And Techniques For IT Managers To Use In Order To Make Innovation Happen In Their Teams

- Staffing Skills IT Managers Must Have: Tips And Techniques That IT Managers Can Use In Order To Correctly Staff Their Teams

- Secrets Of Effective Leadership For IT Managers: Tips And Techniques That IT Managers Can Use In Order To Develop Leadership Skills

- IT Manager Career Secrets: Tips And Techniques That IT Managers Can Use In Order To Have A Successful Career

- IT Manager Budgeting Skills: How IT Managers Can Request, Manage, Use, And Track Their Funding

- Secrets Of Managing Budgets: What IT Managers Need To Know In Order To Understand How Their Company Uses Money

Negotiating

- Getting What You Want In A Negotiation By Learning How To Signal: How To Develop The Skill Of Effective Signaling In A Negotiation In Order To Get The Best Possible Outcome

- Exploring How To Get The Deal That You Want In A Negotiation: How To Develop The Skill Of Exploring What Is Possible In A Negotiation In Order To Reach The Best Possible Deal

- Use The Power Of Arguing To Win Your Next Negotiation: How To Develop The Skill Of Effective Arguing In A Negotiation In Order To Get The Best Possible Outcome

- Learn How To Signal In Your Next Negotiation: How To Develop The Skill Of Effective Signaling In A Negotiation In Order To Get The Best Possible Outcome

- Learn The Skill Of Exploring In A Negotiation: How To Develop The Skill Of Exploring What Is Possible In A Negotiation In Order To Reach The Best Possible Deal

- Learn How To Argue In Your Next Negotiation: How To Develop The Skill Of Effective Arguing In A Negotiation In Order To Get The Best Possible

Outcome|

- How To Open Your Next Negotiation: How To Start A Negotiation In Order To Get The Best Possible Outcome

- Preparing For Your Next Negotiation: What You Need To Do BEFORE A Negotiation Starts In Order To Get The Best Possible Deal

- Learn How To Package Trades In Your Next Negotiation

- All Good Things Come To An End: How To Close A Negotiation - How To Develop The Skill Of Closing In Order To Get The Best Possible Outcome From A Negotiation

- Take No Prisoners In Your Next Negotiation: How To Start A Negotiation In Order To Get The Best Possible Outcome

Miscellaneous

- How To Heal A Broken Leg – Fast!: Understanding how to deal with a broken leg in order to start walking again quickly

- How Software Defined Networking (SDN) Is Going To Change Your World Forever: The Revolution In Network Design And How It Affects You

- The Power Of Virtualization: How It Affects Memory, Servers, and Storage: The Revolution In Creating Virtual Devices And How It Affects You

- The Internet-Enabled Successful School District Superintendent: How To Use The Internet To Boost Parental Involvement In Your Schools

- Power Distribution Unit (PDU) Secrets: What Everyone Who Works In A Data Center Needs To Know!

- Making The Jump: How To Land Your Dream Job When You Get Out Of College!

- How To Use The Internet To Create Successful Students And Involved Parents

"Practical, proven examples of how to use your communication skills to make your product a success!"

> This book has been written with one goal in mind – to show you how to use your communication skills to make your product fly off the shelves. We're going to show you how to make sure that this job turns into a success for you!
>
> **Let's Make Your Career A Success!**

What You'll Find Inside:

- **INTERNET PRODUCT PROMOTION – 4 SECRETS FOR PRODUCT MANAGERS**

- **SEXY ADVERTISING: HOW TO GET YOUR PRODUCT NOTICED**

- **WHY ROI IS THE WRONG WAY TO MEASURE YOUR PRODUCT'S MARKETING PROGRAM**

- **5 SECRETS TO PRODUCT MANGER SUCCESS AT YOUR NEXT TRADE SHOW**

Dr. Jim Anderson brings his 4 college degrees coupled with over 25 years of real-world experience to this book. He's managed products at some of the world's largest firms as well as at start-ups. He's going to show you what you need to do in order to make your career a success!

www.ingramcontent.com/pod-product-compliance
Lightning Source LLC
Chambersburg PA
CBHW061201180526
45170CB00002B/899